But the hour cometh, and now is, when the true worshippers shall worship the Father in spirit and in truth: for the Father seeketh such to worship him.

John 4:23

The Day The Pentecostal Church Died

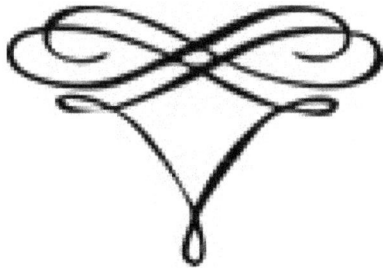

By

Thomas Gilleylen

Evangelist Thomas Gilleylen is married to Missionary Linda Gilleylen. They have seven children and ten grandchildren. They have been married for over 38yrs. They attend the Rose Of Sharon Church of God in Christ in Amory Ms. His mentor was Bishop Charles Harrison Mason.

They can be reached for speaking engagements at
662-825-2707 or tegmason@yahoo.com

Thomas Gilleylen

Table of Content

Thus saith the LORD, Stand ye in the ways, and see, and ask for the old paths, where is the good way, and walk therein, and ye shall find rest for your souls. But they said, we will not walk therein

Jeremiah 6:16

Thomas Gilleylen

There was a time when the term Pentecostal Church carried much weight and power. One knew that they were in the midst of a peculiar praying people. That power has diminished. What happen to the Friday Night Prayer meeting? Where is our mourning bench? Where is our evidence of the Holy Ghost? "The Day the Pentecostal Church Died" takes you down the path of what has been lost, and how to get it back.

Thomas Gilleylen

INTRODUCTION

It's the will of God that I write this book. The Lord inspired me to write in 2012. I have always wanted to write, but could never narrow down exactly what to write about. I love reading about the Pentecostal movement, and have read so many books in my life about them both. I've read the good, the bad, and the ugly.

One subject that fascinated me the most was revivals. I started to read about their developments, and how they were held throughout the world. One of the greatest and most known revival took place after the day of Pentecost in the book of Acts. Another one of my favorites was the Azusa Street revival. It's not my intention to rewrite the history of revivals.

Pentecostal churches were a leading force in the church world, but now it's impact is dwindling. This book is an effort to educate and teach on what must be done to regain that which has been lost. Power must be restored before Christ comes back for his bride.

There have been many great books written by many great authors about past church history and church leaders. History has a habit of repeating itself. There are some Pentecostal churches that are still surviving, but most of them are dead. The leaders can change this picture, and the flock will follow its leaders. The body of Christ is really not Pentecostal. They were given that name by other people because they received the promise on that Jewish holiday.

It takes strong leaders to go against the grain. What you call a Pentecostal church may not be a real Pentecostal church. A good look at the Pentecostal church example will be in the book of Acts. After the day of Pentecost, which is a Jewish feast, the one hundred and twenty was a church family. They all spoke in tongue and stay steadfast in the apostle's doctrine. Fasting and praying was one of the foundations of the early church. The apostles were the leader after Jesus left and went to heaven.

He sent the Holy Ghost to replace himself amongst the disciples. Much of the teaching and information that we have in the Bible after Jesus' death came through revelation by the Apostles and the five-fold ministries. The church was in its first phase in the book of Acts. It was beginning to grow as time went on. Jesus didn't give all the answers to future and oncoming problems, but the Holy Ghost in the Apostles, prophets, and other Christians was able to do the same work that

Jesus did while he was here on earth.

The Holy Ghost was the one that worked through and taught Jesus everything he knew, while on earth. What we must do is very simple. We must go back to the beginning and do our first works over again.

The world makes a big deal about his birth and a very little about his death and resurrection. The death and resurrection were the main purpose of Jesus' being here. They took the pagan "holyday" of Easter and change the true meaning. There is also little teaching about him being fill with the Holy Ghost. He fasted for forty days, was tempted of Satan, and came back in the power of the spirit. From that point on, the gifts of the spirit started to operate in Jesus' ministry.

JESUS IS FIRST

Jesus should be number one in your life. There are many things that can seduce you away from him. This causes you to walk on both sides of the fence. This can kill the life in the church, lukewarm people.

You are a spirit that has a soul living in a natural body. You connect to God with your spirit. You connect to the things of this world with your flesh. This is a conflict that is fighting within you. The pride of life consists of the thing that you value in this life. The things of this world war against the spirit that is in you. This battle will be going on until you leave this world in death or the rapture.

Your number one purpose in life is to love the Lord with all of your spirit, soul, and body. You must study the word of God in order to love Jesus as you should. The two can't be separated. You can't love Jesus without having a strong love for his word.

The scriptures say seek ye first the kingdom of God and all of its righteousness, Matt 6:33. After you read his words on a consistent basis, you must and will start to live by faith, the things that you have learned. The scripture say the just shall live by faith.

FASTING

This is another very important part of the Christian faith and life style. The church died when the church stop fasting. There are many reasons why we should fast. This was an ancient practice before Christ.

We should have a life style of fasting instead of going on special fasts on certain days, like when trouble arises. Both fasts are good, but only one of them will cause you to stay in contact with God. The other method, you are trying to get in touch with God in times of crisis only.

Before Jesus started his ministry, he fasted forty days and forty nights. Then the scriptures say he returned in the power of the spirit. Fasting made the difference in

Jesus' ministry. Fasting also gave him power over all the power of the devil and demonic spirits.

We have this same power over demonic spirit once we give ourselves over to much fasting and prayer. Jesus and the apostles fasted as well as john the Baptist and his disciples. Now days The Pentecostal's love to feast instead of fasting. Foods is involved with everything that we do in church. Mostly every saint is overweight, which causes other health problems. There are natural and spiritual benefits for fasting. Most people belly is their god. If you don't control your appetite, your appetite will control you.

PRAYING

Praying is one of the most important powerful weapons that we have. This is another sign that the church is dying because of the lack of prayer. Prayer and fasting should be done together. Education or no education there is no quarrel with praying. The rich and the poor can operate in this type of ministries.

This was one of Jesus' greatest secrets as the son of God to fulfill his divine calling. This is the only thing that the disciples ask Jesus to teach them to do. They wanted to know how to pray like Jesus prayed. They knew he prayed a lot and long. Sometimes he spent the whole night in prayer.

This was the secret of the Old Testament

prophets. Prayer is a life style and an art that has to be learned and practiced. There are many types of prayer. Roman 8:26 teaches about one type of prayer. Jude 1:20 teaches about another. Ephesians 6:18 teaches about another form of prayer.

Jesus said my house shall be called, the house of prayer for all nations, Isa 56:7. Jesus number one job now is to make intercession for us. Prayer was never taken out of school; it was taken out of some people's heart.

Men who are the leader of their family should be leader in prayer in their home, jobs, churches, communities, and everything else they are involve in or thing they love to do. Civil Rights leaders tried to make changes, by using an example of other world leaders by marching and protesting.

A good example to fight injustice is when God call his leaders like he did in the book of judges. Each leader accomplishes their missions with divine intervention. God was their source of power and not their education, speaking ability, or political connection.

Thomas Gilleylen

STUDYING GOD'S WORD

The Bible says to study to show yourself approved, rightly dividing the word of truth, 2 Tim 2:15. The more you read and study the word, the more you will know the word. This is another sign of the dying church. Going to church is only part of being saved.

Bible study once a week is not enough to keep your spirit man strong on the inside. You must study God's word on a daily basis. The Pentecostal churches died when they replaced the word of God with entertainment, TV, ball games, golf, football, skating, bingo, and other fleshly desires that lust against the spirit. Jesus said man should not live by bread alone, but by every words that proceed out of the mouth of God.

The bible says that the angels obey the voice of the word. God created everything by the word. Jesus said when you speak to your mountain it will obey you. You can use words, to solve all of your problems. Your words are your defense and offence. The weapon that Jesus uses is the word. We will be judged by every idle word that we speak.

The more you know the word of God, the more you will have victory in your life. Your words can be your greatest enemy or your best friend. You should have the word on the inside, to protect you from outside forces.

Death and life are in the power of the tongue. God spoke everything into existence with his word. Satan tried to use the word against Jesus during his temptation in the wilderness after his forty day fast. Jesus fought back with the word. What a fight that must have been. Satan tried to use the word against God in heaven when he tried to take over, but God kick him out. You must be living right for the words to work in your life.

Thomas Gilleylen

WITNESSING

The Pentecostal Church died when they lost the power and the ability to witness. This is not an option. This was a commandment that Jesus gave while he was ascending to heaven. God gave this responsibility to man, not the angels or any other heavenly creature. The church should witness with signs, wonders, and miracles confirming the word.

Dead churches begat dead witnesses with no power to confirm their faith. You must be convincing to yourself before you can convince others. The Bible says he that wins souls must be wise. Jesus said you must be wise as a serpent but harmless as a dove. Witnessing should be a life style for a true saint. Fasting and praying goes before we try to win the lost.

The gifts of the Spirit should be operating in your life to witness properly not your fleshly mind, or your church organization's doctrine that is not scripture based. You must stay full of the Holy Ghost once you have been filled. You should witness everywhere you go, even when you don't feel like it. You should witness in season and out of season. You have been bought with a price. This is a red flag for a dying church.

It is a shame that false prophets take to the street faster than the true witness of God. The true church is locked up in their four walls, witnessing to each other every Sunday.

CASTING OUT DEVILS

The Pentecostal church died when they stopped casting out devils. It was the church reasonability to cast out devils, when it was alive. This is another outward sign that the church has died. Jesus rebuked the disciples for failing to cast out a devil that was in a young man.

They ask Jesus why they couldn't cast the devil out. He said this kind comes out but by fasting and prayer. If the Pentecostals fail to do their job because they don't have the power, they need to take their sign down. It is false advertisement.

The church is powerless when it fails to do its job in deliverance. This is part of the church service that you don't see any more.

Some people think that this is a special ministry, but Jesus said these signs shall follow them that believe. In my name, they shall cast out devils.

You need a prayer life in order to cast out devils. You need to fast also to cast out devils. Casting out devils is an art. Most people at the hospital have demons in them. They can be healed by casting out devils. Devils bring sickness. Changing their bad eating habits, will keep their deliverance.

FRIDAY NIGHT SERVICE

Every Pentecostal church had a special week night service. That service was replaced by entertainment, working two jobs, and sports with friends and family members. That was one of the backbones that made the Pentecostal churches strong.

They wanted to be like other dead churches in the city. They have lost the anointing because they refuse to be different. Some Pentecostal churches had two or three services in a week, not counting Sunday service. They loved God and God's people. Now they attend ballgames instead church services. They love the things of the world instead of God and his work. They love to shop, bowl, visiting their friends, camping,

21

and other fleshly things instead of fellowshipping with the saints.

It is time to get back to the services we once enjoyed. We need to ask God to forgive us for being cold and Luke warm. We need to give him our best and not our leftovers. The preachers must love the house of God so they can convince others to come.

We must prepare ourselves in order to help other when they come. It is not wrong to have some worker on payroll to keep the church open 24/7. You never know who may need help from the church. Church service is important.

PRAYING FOR THE SICK

This is one of the strongest signs of a Pentecostal church when it is alive. The church died when it failed to pray for its member with signs following. You have to love people in order to feel the need of another person. The Pentecostals used to anoint with oil and say the prayer of faith and if you believe you would be heal.

The Bible says the just shall live by faith. You are healed by faith. You must stand on God's words. You must teach healing scriptures to build their faith up. Personal prayer should be done at home before you can pray at church. James said the prayer of faith shall save the sick.

Most people Jesus healed were in the street. The gifts of the spirit should operate anywhere. The church is a good place to get healed, but your gift can operate at the jail house, hospital, or nursing home.

When prayer doesn't work you might have to intercede for the sick person. You should change your bad eating habit sometimes to get healed and to stay healed. There are different method of healing. This is why it is so important to depend on the leading of the Holy Ghost. There is no set rule. Sometime Jesus spoke the word, sometime he used the laying on of hand, and sometime he said your faith had made you whole.

TESTIMONY SERVICE

This is a very important part of church service. Most Pentecostal churches have omitted this part of church services. This has cause death to many churches. In times past, saints had hot testimonies and were on fire. They couldn't wait to get to church to tell about God's goodness. Now you have to beg people to testify with their cold and dead self.

Most church people don't know how to testify without preaching or talking about their problems and bragging about the devil. Good testimony keeps the service moving and keeps people exciting. We have replaced it with praise report, praise team, and praise dancers.

There are other things we do that don't have a strong effect like a good testimony. The leaders in the church should put this back in the church and let these dead and dried up people go back to the altar and get them fill with the Holy ghost.

Now, they use mimic, singing from the choirs, and other time killing methods to keep the people exciting until the dead preacher starts preaching. The Bible says they overcome by the blood of the lamb and the words of their testimony.

LONG VS SHORT SERVICES

Another thing that I have notice that has killed the Pentecostal churches is short services. Most people think that time doesn't matter anymore. Church people's patience is very short at church but very long watching TV, the ballgame, or any other things that excites them.

They can go to work and be there for 8 hours, and then decide to work a double shift and work another 8 hours and think nothing about it. When they go to church, they are in a hurry to get back home to do nothing. What a shame.

There are many reasons for this problem. Some churches are so dead, people can't wait to leave. You have the wrong people in charge. Most Pentecostal churches are just a social club. There is no preparation for the moving of the Spirit. Most pastors and preachers don't even know the bible characters that they are preaching about. The church members love each other at church, but don't know each other away from church.

Jesus said the zeal of my father's house has eating me up. King David loved to spend a long time at God's house. Jesus said my father house shall be called the house of prayer.

SPORT

This is one of the strongest demonic spirits to kill the Pentecostal churches. There are different kinds of sport that can get your child's attention, while they are young. This spirit make the body and soul pull against the spirit in you. Who you feed the most will be the strongest.

The number one problem we have with sport is, we put it before God. We support our children which is good, but when we miss church to support them, that is when we get in trouble. Sport is a god to some people. Sport makes the flesh look good. We look at the strength of the strongest man. We look at the fastest runner. We make gods out of these individuals. The Bible say if any man glory, let him glory in the Lord.

We know more about sports than we know about the Bible. We know the rules, the players of each team and their past history, but we have no idea about the books of the Bible. We don't know the author of each book, when it was written, why it was written, or where it is located in history. We don't even read the most important book in the world, The Bible.

CHURCH DISCIPLINE

The Pentecostal churches died when it failed in church discipline. You must have it at home, school, work, and in the church. The list keeps going about discipline. You must have it within yourself. You must have rules and guidelines for everyone to follow.

When a leader loses respect for God and his words, the people will lose respect for their leaders, church, and the things of God also. Then the people outside will lose respect for that church and its leader. That is why you must have discipline, to keep order and respect.

At one time, if you messed up publicly, you had to repent publicly. Now, most people want to look good for the people, but they forget about God, who sees everything. You shouldn't worry about people and what they think. God is the one that will judge you.

The church should practice discipline also with the Bible as their guide. Your church should have a discipline section for everyone in the church. Stronger discipline should be for the leaders of the church than member. Once they have repented and time has been giving for them to change their behaviors, the church should have open arms to accept them back, to the body of Christ.

CHURCH SHUT-INS

The Pentecostal churches died when they stop what we called shut-ins. Paul called this watching. This was very important for leaders and the saint when they got serious with God. There are some churches that still practice this. Most people don't have a prayer life to be effective on a shut-in.

Apostles Paul calls it watching in 2 Corinthian 6:4-5. King David learned and talked about waiting on the Lord. He developed this skill while he was a lad, keeping the sheep. He went to the temple alone many times waiting on the Lord for instruction. You don't read about king David mother, father, or his brother seeking or waiting on the Lord, but you read a lot about David seeking the Lord in fasting and prayer. He was anointed king and prophet. He was also the anointed Psalter.

He had to have a strong prayer life to hold those offices. He was also the commander in chief for the army. He was a man after God's own heart. What you do in secret God will reward you open. Greater the calling, greater the sacrifice. You must separate from people to get with God. This is hard on the flesh, but it gives you liberty to your spirit. You have to make a decision to die so you can live. You have one life to live, on earth.

DRESS CODE

This is another sign toward the Pentecostal church's death mode. When they started to dress like the world. Your dress code doesn't determine if you are saved or not, but it tells a lot about how a person thinks on the inside. What is in the inside is revealed on the outside. You shouldn't spend so much time trying to impress people from your outward appearance. It is the inner man that you should value and spend time to develop in the image of Christ. Your outward man will return to the dust, but your spiritual man will live forever in heaven or in hell. The choice is yours, not God's.

God believes in equal rights. We go to school for twelve years, and then to college four more years, depending on our major. We do this for the outward man so he can look good to others, but the inner man appearance is hidden from the public eye. The inner man is created in the image of God. When this is done properly, we will dress in a way that will reveal God to the world.

The hair style can reveal your inner condition. Your tight attires reveal your inner condition. The length of your dress is an outward sign of inner trouble. Your excessive jewels reveal also your inner condition.

MONEY

This is another sign that the Pentecostal churches have died. The scripture say that the love of money is the root of all evils. Money is the number one focus and center of attention in most churches. The preachers spend more time at the table during the offering than they do at the altar in prayer.

Jesus said seek the kingdom first, not money or things. It seems like people with the money are the ones to get the most attention, but God looks at the heart. Money reveals the condition of your heart.

It is the anointing that breaks the yoke, not your money. People focus on the dollar bill instead of God words. We need money to live, but we must put it in its proper place, in our life.

Money is a god to some people, like their belly is a god. You should have control over your money and not your money having control over you. Most people have all their faith in the all mighty dollar. We should make the dollar work for us and not us working for the dollar.

Souls should be our number one goal. That is the main reason for the money in the ministries. The more that we have, the more we can do for the Lord. We give too much attention to the offering part of the service. We shouldn't pressure people to give, we should ask. The apostles gave this issue to the deacons, but the preachers and bishops think they can raise more money like Judas. The apostles gave themselves to prayer and to the words of God.

SCHOOL, EDUCATION, COLLEGES AND UNIVERSITY

Another sign that Pentecostal churches have died is they depend on education instead of the anointing and the word of God. You should never use the world's standard to approve or disapprove the God of Abraham, Isaac, and Jacob.

God's wisdom is so much greater than man wisdom. Education without salvation is damnation. God said he has honored his words above his name. Apostle Paul was well educated. History says, he spoke seven different languages. He was a master of religion and was very adamant in his faith. He had one of the greatest teachers of his time. When he learned about Christ, he counted everything as dung.

When he went into Arabian Desert for three years, God gave him a revelation about Christ. He went to Jerusalem and discussed his knowledge with the apostles, who knew the teaching of Christ first hand. They were teaching the same gospel. Your revelation need to be tested by the written word of God. If a person refuse to let his revelation be judged, you should warn such a person that he is out of order.

CHURCH BUILDING

This is another sign that the Pentecostal church has died, when the leaders and the church members spend more time working on the building instead of its members. Most churches spend excess money on the building, after they have drained the people out of their finance. They have all kind of programs in the name of the Lord, to raise money until winning the lost is lost.

Most churches are trying to have a name in the communities instead of having a good name with God. They love to impress people so they can join and help pay for the beautiful edifice they just build with only a few members. Winning souls is not on the agenda anymore. The building fund is the number one topic in the monthly meeting. Fasting and praying is on the back burner.

A new agenda is to raise money to make the church building look good in the community. We need more offices, playgrounds for the children, computers, and anything else to get attention. We need more programs so we can be like other dead churches and to be updated.

The focus has shifted, and the money is very low. The membership has dropped in the last eight months. That is not important right now. We must take care of the church building and forget about everything else. This is another sign of a dead church.

DEACONS

This is another sign that the Pentecostal church has died. This is a killer in the church now. Like everything else, there is a qualification for a deacon. Churches make anyone a deacon that wears pants. He shouldn't have 2 or 3 living wives [like most preachers].The church should have some guide line for this position.

He should be filled with the Holy Ghost with the evidence of speaking in tongue. He should have some wisdom and well-spoken of from the community.

In most church, if you have a little money you can become the head deacon and don't even possess a Bible. Some deacons think they tell the pastor and the preacher what to do. That is another sign that the church is dead.

The deacon should know his Bible like he knows all the players of his favorite football team. He should be able to preach, when the pastor is absent. He should know how to pray and rebuke the devil. He should know how to cast out devils. Raising money is not the only thing he should know how to do.

He should be a man of fasting and prayer also. He shouldn't be involved in the Masonic lodges or other secrets clubs that the Bible condemns. He should not be a drinker or be a gambler.

TRANSPORTATION

Transportation is very important and also a blessing, if you use it the right way. You should own a nice vehicle, but the vehicles shouldn't own you. The saints walked when they didn't have transportation. Now, the Lord has blessed them to purchase new and use vehicles. Even their children have their own vehicles. Some of the saint have their own airplanes.

A real Pentecostal would share their blessing with another saint, who doesn't have any transportation. Some people have made their cars a god. Some vehicles we can't afford but we try to keep up with the joneses. We even try to impress people and make them think we are special by what we drive. God doesn't look at what we drive. He looks at what drives us. We think more about our car than the things of God. This is another sign that the Pentecostal church has died.

Sometimes we talk more about the gift than we do about the giver. If we have the love of God in us, we would ask God to forgive us and deliver us from idol worshipping. We may not be bowing our knees to idols, but we can have an idol in our heart for materials things.

CHILDREN

Another sign that the Pentecostal church is dead was when we stopped training our children up as they should be. We let the world, celebrities, and demonic television programs replace the parent's job.

We don't spend enough time with them because we husbands work so much and the wife is busy working also. We use daycares and other worldly care center to poison our children. We even let the church raise them.

Sometime our understanding of scriptures is different from some church member. You are the only person that is capable of raising your own children. The educational system is totally against what the Bible says about ninety percent of the subject.

The media gives a fatal attraction on life itself. They praise drugs, sex, crime, sport and other false hope in this excitement of the flesh. Children give so much of their time in these events, and can't spend over two hours in church without complaining. This comes from poor home training. This is a true sign that the Pentecostal church has died.

We used to have revival for one to two months. Now we have them for a few days. We used to raise our children up in this type of environment. Now they tell us when they want to attend and when they don't want to attend. This is another red flag.

STUDY WHAT TO PREACH FOR THE CHURCH

Another sign that the Pentecostal church has died, is the fact that preachers already know they're going to preach before they arrive at church. They depend on books, CDs' and other mean of information instead of praying through, until you get the answer in prayer.

Sometimes they would watch a good preacher on television and steal their sermon, because they are too lazy to seek the Lord for their own sermon for that day. You can go to the internet and get all of your sermons and the background information that goes with it, but only God know what the saints need.

You can study the Hebrew, Greek and other material on the Bible, but what you need is revelation and not so much fancy information and big words. This comes with a fasting and prayer life. You must prepare yourself before you prepare your sermons. After you have studied the Bible, You can ask the Lord about the message for that day and night service. He might give the message to someone else. Everyone in church must be ready. The Bible is the number one guide for your life. You must read it daily for it to have an impact on your life.

FIVE FOLD MINISTRY

This is another sign that the Pentecostal church has died. They don't operate or believe in the fivefold ministries. Ephesians 4:11 explains this in detail, but the organized church has denied these offices. God had put apostles first and then Prophets. These are foundation gifts for churches. We also have the pastor, evangelist, and teachers. We hear lots of talk about false prophets but, there is more false pastors compared to false prophets.

We can't operate properly if we disobey these scriptures on this subject. There are some ministries that acknowledge these offices because they have a better understanding of these scriptures. They spend time in prayer and fasting. The same way you were trained as a new member, you need to be retrain about these offices. They have not been done away with.

The enemy fears these offices. The churches need a mentorship course, instead of colleges, to understand God and his operation. You are called from birth by God for the 5 fold Ministries. You can't be voted in. Your money can't buy you into these offices.

Bishop Charles H. Mason was the founder of the Church of God in Christ. He also was an apostle that God raise to birth the Church Of God in Christ. The signs of apostles follow his ministry until his death. He also stated that a bishop can't appoint a pastor over a church. That is the job of an apostle, which mean, he still believe that there are apostles and prophets in the church. Most of

his teaching has been lost in the church that
God use him to organize.

Thomas Gilleylen

GIFTS OF THE SPIRIT

This is another great sign that the Pentecostal church has died. What made the Pentecostal churches so powerful and different from all other churches? The Gifts of the spirit was very strong in every church. You may be rich or poor, it made no difference. You can be educated or uneducated. Your color made no difference. It didn't matter where you were from.

The gifts of the spirit are what made Jesus ministry supernatural. He was the Son of God, but he didn't operate as the Son of God. He operated in the Holy Ghost. He left us an example to follow. He told the disciples to follow his instruction and receive the promise. He ordered them not to leave Jerusalem. Jesus gave his last commandment in the book of Acts the first chapter before he left. 1 Cor 12th chapter explain the nine gift of the spirit, that should be operating in your church by all of its members. The bible says that we should desire for these gifts in 1 Cor 14th chapter. Jesus left us an example how the gifts should be operating in 1 Cor 12th chapter. Once you receive the gift of the Holy Ghost and speak in tongue, you are ready for the gifts of the spirit to operate in you.

VOTING AND POLITICS

Another sign that the Pentecostal church has died, is the preachers and church members get tied up in politics instead of ministry. People think voting certain people in office will make a big change in their churches.

Pentecostal's used to put their trust in God and his words, but now they trust the politicians. This is a true sign of weakness for God's chosen people. You will get in trouble every time. God wanted to be king, judge, and everything else, but the people wanted a man. Now we are educated and we are smarter than the one who made us. We have more confidence in the government and everyone else who seems to be a qualified person. When God's people need deliverance, he would send a prophetic person. God didn't look how well you were educated. He was looking at your heart.

We look at the NAACP and other human organization instead of God and the ones that he uses. There are many agencies that we can use and trust, but I believe that we must put God first and use the others last, as God directs us. You can't use human methods, to fight spiritual warfare.

UNEQUALLY YOKED

This is another sign that the Pentecostal church has died, they are marring unsaved people, people who don't believe like they do. You should never marry a person who believes in Christ, but doesn't believe in the Bible as the one true word of God.

Something is wrong when you desire to be with a person that desires the things of the world and worldly people instead of Godly saints. Something is wrong with that picture. You shouldn't break the scriptures to fulfill the lust of the flesh. You must take control of your flesh and the desires it has. The scripture asked the question, what has light to do with darkness. They don't have anything in common. You are heading for trouble when you start loving worldly people and spending your time with them instead godly people.

A saved person shouldn't be dating an unsaved person. You can be religious and don't know God or Jesus, not to even mention the Holy Ghost.

Preachers should have a standard and a guide line to follow instead of being like the world. Most preachers don't want to offend, and they are looking for new ways to gain new members.

We need to teach our children about the occult and about other false religions that are not scripturally sound. God's word should be the measuring stick that we use for our policy in church. Just because a law was passed doesn't mean it is right in God eyes. Woman was made for man, not man made for man. Judgment will follow these type of activities.

CONCLUSION

Let's hear the conclusion of the whole matter. The church must go back to the basics which comes from the book of Acts. After they received the baptism of the Holy Ghost with the evidence of speaking in tongues, members received power.

Many churches have failed to follow these founding fathers' beliefs and practices. Most pastors don't want to offend anyone. The leaders are looking to have a mega church and a big choir. They are looking for a big offering, pastor anniversaries, and other church gimmicks to raise money in the name of the Lord.

We must follow 2 chronicles 7:14 If my people, which are called by my name, shall humble themselves, and pray, and seek my face, and turn from their wicked ways; then will I hear from heaven, and will forgive their sin, and will heal their land.

This is a good place to get started. In Psalms 16:7, it says I will bless the LORD, who hath given me counsel: my reins also instruct me in the night seasons. King David spent many nights in the temple waiting on the Lord to give him instructions as a king. Act 13th chapter reveal how the Holy Ghost was giving instruction as the apostles fasted and prayed until the Holy Ghost start speaking.

We love to shout and dance, but we must seek the Lord first and then obey the leading of the holy ghost instead of leaders who are wanting to be popular in the community.

Now is the time to seek the Lord like never before. If a person makes up their mind to serve God, he would be a changed man. One man can change a city, town, or state. A good woman working with him can cause him to double his work in the Lord. Will you be that one man or woman that God is looking for? Now is the acceptable time to give yourself to God like never before. Your reward will be great in heaven.

Thomas Gilleylen

www.ingramcontent.com/pod-product-compliance
Lightning Source LLC
LaVergne TN
LVHW041206080426
835508LV00008B/827